Rachel's Little Quote Book

Messages She Left Us

Jan Myers
at www.RachelsRanch.org

Rachel's Little Quote Book
By Jan Myers at www.RachelsRanch.org
Copyright ©2011 Jan Myers
First Edition: April, 2011

Notice of Rights
All rights reserved. No part of this book may be reproduced, stored in a retrieval system, or transmitted in any form or by any means, without the prior written permission of the publisher, except in the case of brief quotations embedded in critical articles or reviews.

Contact the Author
Jan Myers may be contacted at **www.RachelaRanch.org**.

Donate to the Camp at Rachel's Ranch
We invite you to contribute to the building of the Camp at Rachel's Ranch – Rachel's dream – to benefit abused and disadvantaged children ages 8 to 16 at **www.RachelsRanch.org** .

First Printing, 2011
ISBN 978-0615469065
Printed in the United States of America

Dedication
To Rachel

I thought of you with love today,
but that is nothing new.
I thought about you yesterday,
and the day before that, too.
I think of you in silence,
I often say your name,
But all I have are memories
and your picture in a frame.
Your memory is my keepsake
with which I'll never part.
God has you in his keeping,
I have you in my heart.

I shed tears for what might have been,
a million times I've cried.
If love alone could have saved you,
you never would have died.
In life I loved you dearly,
in death I love you still,
In my heart you hold a place
no one could ever fill.
It broke my heart to lose you,
but you didn't go alone,
For part of me went with you,
the day God took you home
—Unknown.

Contents

Introduction	Page 7
Section 1: Quotes From Rachel's Little Quote Book	Page 11
Section 2: Quotes From Rachel Herself	Page 91
Conclusion	Page 105
About the Author	Page 106
Coming Soon	Page 110
How You Can Help Build the Camp at Rachel's Ranch	Page 111

Introduction

This book is written without apology as a tribute to the life and goodness of Rachel Ann Carr. Rachel was a beautiful, loving, and significant woman. Terms used to describe her in a Discovery workshop, handwritten on small slips of white paper and framed in her bedroom, were: *beauty, warm love, friendship, hope, faith, compassion, love, friendship, big heart, loving, and beautiful heart.*

It was June 26, 2010. Rachel was just 26 years old.

When I saw Dave's name on the screen of Larry's cell phone that Saturday morning, I was so excited that Dave was calling from his Army training in Virginia that I grabbed for the phone.

Little did I know that our lives would be forever changed by Daves' words, "Rachel was killed in a car wreck last night." What? Who was killed? No! How could we live without our Rachel?

It wasn't just family that was devastated, but so many friends and co-workers, many of whom she referred to as "my kids" over her 11 years with Gap.

After the candlelight vigil the following night at the Banana Republic in Allen, Texas where Rachel worked as a store manager, many of the employees asked for the opportunity to see Rachie's apartment, to see the other side of this wonderful person they loved and appreciated.

And so we traveled to her home, through the intersection where she had been killed the night before by a driver going 110 mph, and then just two more blocks to her apartment.

Everyone walked through to see the things that were uniquely Rachel – her many photos and decorations, her clock collection, her button collection, and her collection of quotes found all around her apartment, on the walls, the mirrors, the refrigerator, and on photos.

Rachel was always looking for ways to improve herself, to find the most in life, to deal with her past and to be the best person she could be.

This collection of Rachel's quotes is a reflection of these desires. It is also a source of continuing inspiration she has left for all of us.

Just last week I was in Dallas and stopped by the Allen Banana Republic to visit Rachel's friends and co-workers. The memorial they made to her is still in their work room and while visiting, several of them told me that when things aren't going right for them, they simply stop and ask themselves, "What would Rachel do?" Then they get started doing it.

I, too, find myself often wondering, "What would Rachel do?"

On April 27, 2010, just two months before her death, Rachel wrote the following at a workshop:

My mission: *encourage love and self-worth in everyone I meet.*

My vision: *uplift people around me, be kind, understanding, encouraging, and bring compliments.*

What do I want to work on first? *make someone smile every day.*

Within this book you will not find all the quotes Rachel loved throughout her life. She tended to collect them in small notebooks and when a book was full, she would throw it away and begin a new one.

So these are her final quotes written in her last little quote book, Rachel's final words to us to live by until we meet her again.

It is my hope that we can all learn from these quotes what Rachel would have us learn and apply it to our lives and our relationships as she did. She would want us to.

We will honor Rachel's memory if we, too, attempt to live her mission, vision and goal.

Whose face will wear a smile today because of you?

Section 1: Quotes from Rachel's Little Quote Book

Quote 1

I can choose to indulge in my frustrations or I can choose to create a habit of happiness. It's not easy, but it's worth the fight.
--John Mayer

This was one of two quotes written in marker on Rachel's bathroom mirror when she died.

It was Rachie's daily reminder that she could make a conscious choice to create happiness with each step she took, wherever life took her that day. Her last day on earth she had done just that. And it was a happy day for her.

Quote 2

> # Let it be.
> --Stephanie Fitzgerald

This was the other quote on Rachel's bathroom mirror when she died. Rachel had a great admiration for Stephanie whom she met through the Discovery workshops. There was something in Rachel's life that she needed to put behind her and Stephanie was influential in helping Rach to "let it be" and move on with creating happiness in her life and the lives of those around her.

Quote 3

Combination of factors, really.

Uh, no clean clothes.

*--Julia Roberts
as Anna Scott Notting Hill*

Quote 4

Trust everyone, but always brand your cattle.

--Unknown

Quote 5

I really believe that everything is meant to be. You can't ask, "Why is this happening to me?" It's happening to you! Life's tough. Get a helmet.

--Jennifer Aniston
Vogue, April, 2006

Quote 6

If you don't make waves, no one will know you've been swimming.

--Real Simple Magazine

Quote 7

And yet, to say the truth, reason and love keep little company together nowadays.

--William Shakespeare
A Midsummer Night's Dream,
Act III, Scene 1

Quote 8

> *Sarcasm is the refuge for people who know they are wrong and are on the ropes.*
>
> *--Sally Field as Nora "Brothers and Sisters"*

Quote 9

Stop waiting for others to love me first.

--Wild at Heart

Quote 10

I can affirm this: even though I have never been there . . . the moon is not exactly a potato.

--Salvador Dali

Quote 11

Don't ask yourself what the world needs. Ask yourself what makes you come alive, and go do that.

--Gil Bailie

Quote 12

Let us step out into the night and pursue that flighty temptress, adventure.

*--Albus Dumbledore
Harry Potter 6*

Quote 13

People, even more than things, have to be restored, revived, reclaimed, and redeemed; never throw out anyone.

--Audrey Hepburn

Quote 14

Love is but the discovery of ourselves in others, and the delight in the recognition.

--Alexander Smith

Quote 15

I believe in hard work and luck, and that the first often leads to the second.

J.K. Rowling

Quote 16

This will all make perfect sense someday. I'll be A-OK. I don't understand the numbers but my faith is in the math. And the odds are all this pain will even out in the end and we'll all look back and laugh. And to all the hearts I've broken and the ones who once broke mine, I've got suspicions all will be forgiven in time. All you gotta do is call them up and say ... There's got to be a reason for the rain. And if it ever gets bad, I mean really bad, I'll move to Nova Scotia and forget the life I've had.

--John Mayer, Perfect Sense

Quote 17

What you feel only matters to you. It's what you do to the people you say you love that's what matters. It's the only thing that counts.

--The Last Kiss

Quote 18

Sometimes I feel the fear of uncertainty stinging clear. And I can't help but ask myself how much I let the fear take the wheel and steer.

--Incubus, Drive

Quote 19

But this morning there was a calm I can't explain. Rock candy's melted; only diamonds now remain.

--John Mayer
Clarity

Quote 20

All I want is for you to be happy. Take this woman and make you my family. Finally you have found someone perfect. Finally you have found yourself.

--Red Hot Chili Peppers
Hard to Concentrate

Quote 21

The more I see, the less I know, the more I like to let it go.

*--Red Hot Chili Peppers
Snow*

Quote 22

*When I smile I'm a really smile.
I got dreams so wide like a country mile.*

*--Red Hot Chili Peppers
Make You Feel Better*

Quote 23

Would you want me when I'm not myself? Wait it out while I am someone else?

--John Mayer
Not Myself

Quote 24

It's good to be scared. It means you still have something to lose.

--Grey's Anatomy Chief

Quote 25

*Look for the ridiculous
in everything and
you will find it.*

--Jules Renard, 1890

Quote 26

I believe that my life's gonna see the love I give returned to me.

--John Mayer

Quote 27

But she did love him. I believe it. I know exactly how that is, to love somebody who doesn't deserve it. Because they are all you have. Because any attention is better than no attention.

--*Augusten Burroughs*
Running with Scissors

Quote 28

Sometimes you need to go backward in order to go forward. You need to understand where you've been in order to make any sense of where you are.

--Jan Stanton Hitchcock
Social Crimes

Quote 29

If a girl looks swell when she meets you, who gives a damn if she's late? Nobody.

--J.D. Salinaer

Quote 30

It's better to be hated for who you are than be loved for who you're not.

--Andre Gide

Quote 31

If you do what you've always done, you'll get what you've always got.

--Discovery Banner

Quote 32

Or here's a radical concept: Maybe I can stop interrupting others when they are speaking because no matter how creatively I try to look at my habit of interrupting, I can't find another way to see it than this: I believe that what I am saying is more important than what you are saying! And I can't find another way to see that than "I believe that I am more important than you." And that must end!

--Eat, Pray, Love
Page 193

Quote 33

I know that by holding on each moment, each hour, each day, the days add up each week, each month. If I hold on I will be fine.

--A Million Little Pieces

Quote 34

There is nothing more important than today.

--Discovery Banner

Quote 35

All our dreams can come true if we have the courage to pursue them.

--Walt Disney

Quote 36

See, now that's your problem. You're wishin' too much, Baby. You gotta stop wearing your wishbone where your backbone outta be.

--Eat, Pray, Love
Page 150

Quote 37

If you want crappy things to stop happening to you, then stop accepting crap and demand something more.

--Christina Yang
Grey's Anatomy

Quote 38

The truth is not full of fact or reason – it's just what everyone agrees on.

--Wicked

Quote 39

For some reason, I feel the same way about you that I felt about my kids when they were small—that it wasn't their job to love me, it was my job to love them.

--Eat, Pray, Love
Page 311

Quote 40

*Tell the truth,
tell the truth,
tell the truth.*

--Sheryl Louise Moller

Quote 41

Significance.

--Stephanie Powell

Quote 42

The shell must break before the bird can fly.

--Tennyson

Quote 43

Growing up means giving up everything that makes you happy.

--Marge Simpson (when she takes away Maggie's pacifier)

Rachel loved the Simpsons beginning as a little girl when her Bart Simpson earrings were her favorites. On her Facebook list of "16 Things You Might Not Know About Me," Rachel wrote:

"#14- My first grade picture is of me with a cute little girl bob, straight bangs across my forehead, pink T and blue flowered vest, and Bart Simpson earrings. The Simpsons had only been on for a year. How cool was I in first grade?"

Quote 44

If you can make a girl laugh, you can make her do anything.

--Marilyn Monroe

Quote 45

Duct tape makes you smart.

--Burn Notice

Quote 46

You can try to say to a rainbow, "Hey, be more like a cloud." But it's only ever gonna be a 7-colored cloud.

--John Mayer

Quote 47

Learn what is important and laugh at the rest.

--Hermann Hesse

Quote 48

> *I get up. I walk. I fall down. Meanwhile, I keep dancing.*
>
> *-Hillel*

Quote 49

God save me from my friends. I can protect myself from my enemies.

--Marechal Villars (leaving Louis XIV)

Quote 50

I see you, the only one who knew me. But now your eyes see through me. I guess I was wrong. So what now?

--Deep Blue Something
Breakfast at Tiffany's

Quote 51

Or would it mean anything if you knew what I'm left imagining in my mind?

--Billie Myers
Kiss the Rain

Quote 52

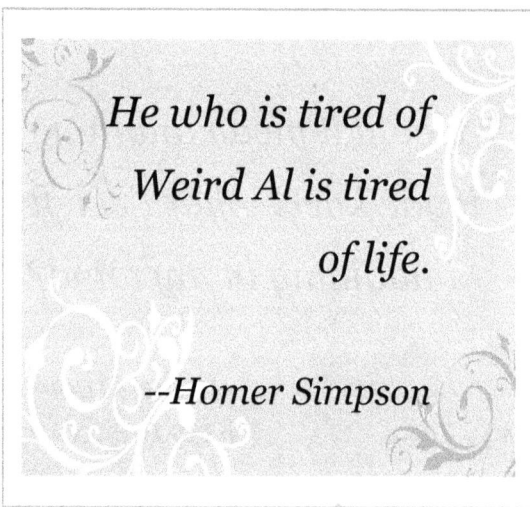

He who is tired of Weird Al is tired of life.

--Homer Simpson

On Rachel's list of "16 Things You Might Not Know About Me" on her Facebook page, she wrote:

> "#2- I think Homer Simpson is one of the smartest men ever. "

Just love her humor!

Quote 53

Joking is a disguised request for approval – that's saying, "Joke, but really love me."

--I Heart Huckabees

Quote 54

Nelson has never steered me wrong, Honey. Nelson is gold.

--Homer Simpson

Quote 55

Always speak the truth because others will hold you in high esteem as a person who can be trusted.

--Sherrie L. Householder

Quote 56

> *Forgiveness is knowing that love is the answer to all questions.*
>
> --Judith Mammay

Quote 57

Get in touch with the person you want to be and become that. Listen to your heart . . . you can find the answer there to every question you have.

--Donna Fargo

Quote 58

Life is good, love is powerful, and the future is full of promise.

--Anonymous

Quote 59

Even when you feel as though there isn't a lot you can do to change unhappiness or problems, you can always do a little – and <u>a little at a time eventually makes a big difference.</u>

--Barbara Cage
(Underline added by Rachel.)

Quote 60

If you celebrate only the most spectacular events, you'll spend a lot of time waiting for happiness to find you.

--Patty J. Rice

Quote 61

Finish every day and be done with it. You have done what you could. Some blunders and absurdities no doubt crept in; forget them as soon as you can. Tomorrow is a new day; begin it well and serenely and with too high a spirit to be cumbered with your old nonsense. This day is all that is good and fair. It is too dear, with its hopes and invitations, to waste a moment on the yesterdays.

--Ralph Waldo Emerson

Quote 62

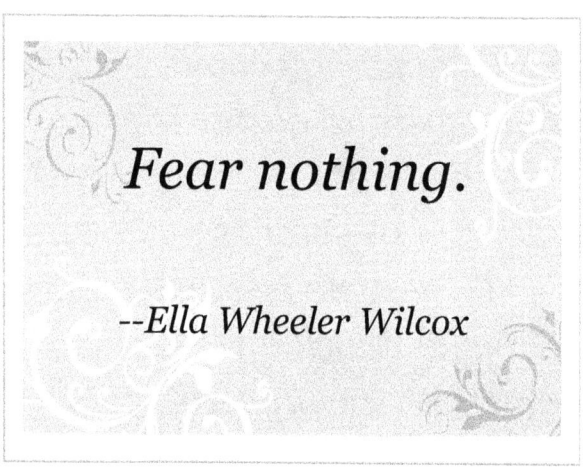

Quote 63

If you have a dream, then – by all means – do what it takes to make it come true.

--Collin McCarty

Quote 64

There is nothing either good or bad, but thinking makes it so.

--William Shakespeare

Quote 65

If you clear out all that space in your mind that you're using right now to obsess about this guy, you'll have a vacuum there, an open spot – a doorway. And guess what the universe will do with that doorway? It will rush in – God will rush in – and fill you with more love than you ever dreamed.

---Eat, Pray, Love
Page 150

Quote 66

Hang in there ... and take care to see that you don't lose sight of the one thing that is constant, beautiful, and true: Everything will be fine.

--Douglas Pagels

Quote 67

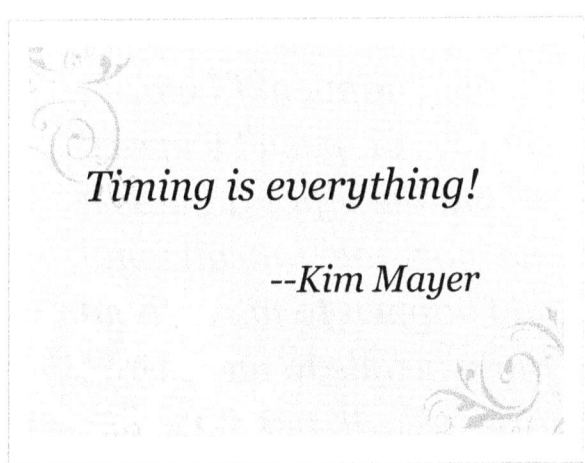

Quote 68

Maybe I was scared of what would happen if I wasn't there . . . I wasn't worried about the office. I guess it was more me. I mean what would happen to me without those people to please and those tasks to get done, like maybe those were the things holding me together and without them I would fall apart?

—Toni Collette
In Her Shoes

Quote 69

It's only after you've lost everything that you're free to do anything.

*--Brad Pitt as Tyler
In Fight Club*

Quote 70

Well-behaved women rarely make history.

--Laurel Thatcher Ulrich

Quote 71

I don't really care if my glass is half-full or half-empty. I'm just happy to have a glass.

--Joe Farrell

Quote 72

*If you pray for rain,
be prepared to deal
with some mud.*

--Anonymous

Quote 73

Why not climb out on a limb? That's where the fruit is.

--Mark Twain

Quote 74

Go confidently in the direction of your dreams. Live the life you've imagined.

--Henry David Thoreau

Quote 75

Life isn't about waiting for the storm to pass. It's about learning to dance in the rain.

--Unknown

Quote 76

A weed is no more than a flower in disguise.

--James Russell Cowell

Quote 77

*Be the kind of woman that when you get up in the morning the devil says:
"Oh, crap, she's up!"*

--Anonymous

Quote 78

Love without honesty is hypocrisy. Honesty without love is brutality.

--Warren Wiersbe

Section 2 – Quotes from Rachel, Herself

Following are a few of the things we remember Rachel saying often, and now we find ourselves fondly quoting her.

Quotes from Rachel, Herself
Quote 1

Cry me a river,

build a bridge,

and get over it!

--Rachel Carr

About the time Rachie was in college, she expanded on a slang saying we often used in our family. When someone – on tv, a movie, or in real life – would be complaining about something, we would usually say, "Oh, cry me a river!"

So by the time Rach was in college, when similar circumstances occurred, Rach expanded on our saying and taught us this quote.

Rachel often said that wasn't original to her, but to her family it was ---so we adopted it as our own.

Quotes from Rachel, Herself
Quote 2

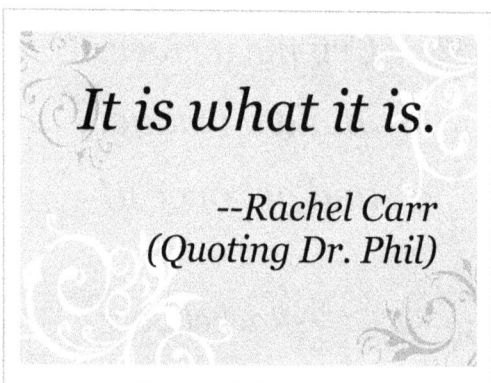

This quote was submitted by Rachel's co-workers and friends at the Banana Republic store in the Allen Outlet Mall in Allen, Texas. It was Rachie's way of saying, "Just deal with it and move on."

The managers at BR told me, "We say it for her every day!"

Quotes from Rachel, Herself
Quote 3

If you build it, they will come.

--Rachel Carr
Quoting a line from
"Field of Dreams"

Jill Pennell, Rachel's friend and co-worker, remembers that during the really tough times in the store – preparing for "Black Friday" (the day following Thanksgiving), or tax-free week, or the friends and family promotion—when preparations for the big event became stressful and demanding, Rachel encouraged the employees by saying, "If you build it they will come."

Quotes from Rachel, Herself
Quote 4

> *Believe in something, as long as it teaches you to be a better person.*
>
> *--Rachel Carr*
> *Posted under "Religion" on Rachel's Facebook page*

'Nuff said!

Although Rachel had a very strong faith in our Savior, Jesus Christ, and in our Heavenly Father, she accepted people for who they are and what they believe. She didn't try to change them, nor did she simply tolerate them. Rachel fully looked for and embraced the goodness in others.

Quotes from Rachel, Herself
Quote 5

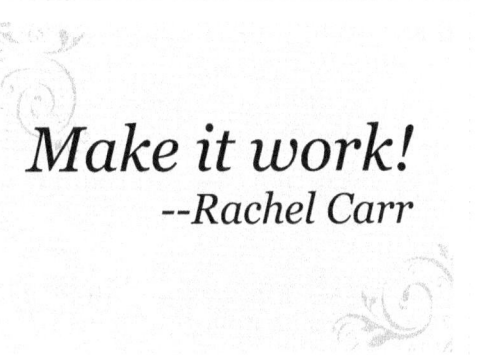

Make it work!
--Rachel Carr

The following letter was written to me by Harlee Cochran, a co-worker of Rachel's at Banana Republic, just two months after Rachel's death:

"Mrs. Myers! I wanted to share something with you. I am applying for college and I had to write an essay for TCU. The topic was: 'Write about someone who has made an impact in your life.'

For a while I was stuck. I didn't know what to write about and then, like a light bulb, it just hit me: Rachel. Rachel made a huge impact on me!
I wanted to share my essay with you, so here it is.

'**Make it work!**' That's what my manager, Rachel Carr, always told me when I didn't know how to make something happen. Rachel was the kind of person who made you think for yourself. She passed away this year, and before then, I had no idea what kind of impact she had on me.

She would always tell me, 'I'm hard on you because I know how good you can truly be.' I used to hear that at least twice a day, every day. I never comprehended the things she said and did most of the time, at least not until I didn't hear them anymore.

I now say to myself when something isn't going the way I want it to, 'Make it work!'

Rachel changed my life because she never let me be less than what she thought I could be. Rachel has always been important to me. She made me a better person by just being herself.

Our Banana Republic family has a saying: 'When I grow up, I want to be just like Rachel!' And it is so true. If I can even be half the woman Rachel was, I will be satisfied. She made an amazing impact in my life and I am forever grateful.

I hope you know that you raised an amazing woman, and I know I wouldn't be the person I am today without a push from Rach. I still think about you and your family and my heart goes out to y'all. I hope this made you smile. ;-) Harlee"

Rachel's 16 Things You May, or May Not, Know About Me (from her Facebook page)

For Rachel C- (not Manager Rachel :))
by Rachel Carr on Wednesday, November 26, 2008

1- I really believe that Cranberry Sauce (from the can) is the reason that we celebrate Thanksgiving.
2- I think Homer Simpson is one of the smartest men ever.
3- I write down quotes on little bits of paper all the time, and then collect them into a silly little notebook, which I discard and redo every couple of years.
4- I love post-its of all sizes.
5- I like anything that reminds me of being a little girl. For example, I really like sparklers, candy cigarettes, and Ritz crackers.
6- I believe that my best quality is my unconditional loyalty, but it is also the quality that causes me the most sadness.
7- I love lazy rivers at water parks, but I am so freaked out by touching strangers' hair that is no longer attached to their heads that I refuse to go in the lazy rivers any more.

8- I desperately want a new set of Lego's, but I am afraid that everyone will laugh at me, so I keep refusing to buy them. When I was a little girl, I had pink, purple, and white Legos and I loved them.

9- I always cheer for the underdog, but then I get really sad when they win because that means that the favorite lost. I just want everyone to win all the time.

10- I think white tulips are the prettiest things on the entire planet.

11- I never order my own drinks. I will drink anything that is ordered for me, but if the only option is to order for myself, I just don't drink. Is that weird?

12- I don't understand the Post Office. Or Electricity. Or City Buses. I refuse to ride them without assistance from someone who is experienced.

13- My underwear and my bra need to match in a sense. Not that they need to match, really, but they surely can't clash. It just freaks me out.

14- My first grade picture is of me with a cute little girl bob, straight bangs across my forehead, pink T and blue flowered vest, and Bart Simpson earrings. The Simpsons had only been on for a year. How cool was I in first grade?

15- When the weather changes, my skin gets dry.

And when my skin gets dry, I get itchy. Then I scratch, and scratch, and scratch. And pretty soon, I scratch so much that I have scabs. I am slightly obsessive.

16- When things are really important, I write them down on my hand. That is the only way I can stop obsessing about stuff. If I don't write it down on my hand, I can't be held responsible for remembering.

Rachel's 25 Things About Me (from her Facebook page)

25 Things About Me (not including the 16 from before) by **February 2, 2009**

1- I have always wanted a pond in my front yard with a flock of 13 flamingos.
2- I have secretly wanted to be a smoker since I was a small child. It just looks cool.
3- I am attracted to EVERY man I meet with brown eyes and brown hair who is over 5'11". If he could make me laugh in the first minute, its love at first sight. And if said man had an Irish accent, I would never love another man ever.
4- I want to have a green thumb so badly that it hurts. But, all my life I have killed plants, beginning with my first cactus at age 5.
5- I am going to get married in Vegas (I call it eloping with invitations) and I want to be proposed to on a Wednesday without a ring.
6- When I was in 4th grade, I began my love affair with Jim Carey. I put up a poster of him in Batman Forever on my bedroom door, and wouldn't allow anyone to touch it. To this day, the memory of him is the biggest reason I like Batman movies.
7- I am old inside. Think about it. Don't you think I have been a 40 year old woman since before you met

me?

8- I desperately want to be a soccer mom. Seriously.

9- Every time I tell someone what my favorite restaurant is, they laugh. And there are only 3 people I know who will go there without whining. They just know it is my favorite, and they accept me for who I am.

10- I think there is a mouse that lives in my pantry. And now I knock on the pantry door to make sure he knows I am coming in.

11- I LOVE LOVE LOVE orange soda from McDonald's. I hate grape soda from anywhere.

12- I don't take showers. I don't believe in them.

13- Most of the time when you are talking to me, I am wiggling my fingers in a certain order. And I can't stop. And it probably means that I am not listening to you at all.

14- I BELIEVE that my right side is superior to my left. And it's not because I am right handed. IT IS BETTER.

15- I am constantly counting my teeth with my tongue.

16- I refuse to fold my own clothing. I hang up some, but usually just leave them all in a pile.

17- I love Galveston, and everything about it.

18- I am banned from playing Tetris, or any block game like it. I get addicted, and then I play so long that I see it when I close my eyes at night. I can't fall asleep because I am playing out hypothetical situations. And I am not even any good to begin with.

19- I have always believed that I would move back to Houston some day. I love and miss the trees and vegetation.

20- I would estimate that 25% of the things that come out of my mouth are lines from a movie or TV show that I stole. So when you see me smiling, staring off into space, and laughing creepily to myself, I am really remembering something you probably never saw.

21- I hate the cold. And by cold, I mean anything under 78 degrees.

22- I am the most sentimental person you know.

23- I can't remember half the things that I should because my brain is full of the secrets to Mario World.

24- I have been carrying the same lunch bag since 2004. It is actually a Trick-or-Treat bag that looks like a mummy, and it is called "The Boo Bag."

25- My favorite color has been grey for about three years now. It started because I went to work somewhere that had a no-color policy in the dress code. And it stuck because now all of my clothes match all of the time.

Conclusion

Rachel took the time to write down each of the quotes in her little quote book because they had meaning to her in her life. I hope that at various times in your life each of them may mean something to you, too, and inspire you to be the person Rachel would hope you would be.

I'll always believe this is one of Rachel's ways of continuing to talk with us and teach us.

Thank you for purchasing this book of quotes. Your support of our project to build the *Camp at Rachel's Ranch* to honor Rachel's memory and fulfill her dream means a great deal to us.

And please remember that April is National Child Abuse Prevention Month. Please do what you can to break the silence of abuse and help the children speak up and receive help.

About the Author

In reality, the author of this book is Rachel. I have merely pulled together for her the quotes she collected the last year or two of her life to share with you. So let me tell you about my co-author, Rachel Ann Carr.

Rachel likely never realized that in collecting this last book of quotes she was contributing to a book that would be published without her input. Each quote she wrote in her little quote book was important to her and taught her a life lesson, made her think, or just boosted her spirits.

Both Rachel's grandmother and I (her mother) love to write, but Rachel had the most writing talent in our family. Rach and I talked about how fun it would be one day for us to write children's books together. Unfortunately, that's one of the many things we will not get to enjoy doing.

Following Rachel's death, the District Attorney's office gave us a book titled, *"No Time for Goodbyes."* It's an excellent book for families who suffer the sudden loss of a loved one, usually due to crime. The book includes the following quote:

> *When you lose your parents,*
> *you lose your past.*
> *But when you lose your child,*
> *you lose your future*
>
> *--Janice Harris Lord*
> *No Time for Goodbyes.*

And I find this to be so true when I think of all the things Rachel, Larry and I still planned for our future, including writing those children's books. Although this is not a children's book, Rachel and I have written it together, for which I am grateful.

Rachel was just 26 when she was killed on June 26, 2010, on her way home from work. Rachel was creative and intelligent. She skipped two grades in school and was accepted at a major university at the age of 16. She excelled in her management role and had just begun her 11th year with Gap, Inc., starting as a clerk at age 16, and was a manager when she died. At her candlelight vigil held the day after her death at her Banana Republic store, Larry and I were told Rachel "was their rising star."

Rachel was a beautiful young woman who gave so much to others. Often she would ask, "What's in your heart?" She wanted to know what was important to people. She never saw race, size, or sexual orientation or lifestyle. What she saw was the goodness in each individual.

Rachel's Facebook page describes Rachel in her own words:

"I like my puppies and my kitty. They make me happy. I never give up on anyone. I collect buttons, clocks, pigs, elephants, and Sharpies. I love John. I like books. I am super funny to myself. I like to take care of people."

And "take care of people" she did!

For the last couple of years before her death, Rachel often talked about her plans to take care of her dad and I in our old age. We thought we'd live next to each other, Larry and I in one house and Rach and her husband and children next door. She wanted to be a great mom and have a bunch of boys she could take to all their ball games. She was so excited at the thought of being a "soccer mom." And she wanted to host summer camps for abused kids.

Rachel herself had a difficult childhood feeling abandoned by her natural father, a loss she never understood and only overcame two months before her death, but was dearly loved by her stepfather. At the age of six she was molested by a family friend. This was the genesis of her desire to help abused children and young adults. Rachel actively participated in child abuse prevention and hoped to someday have a summer camp for kids where, as Rach would say, "they can just be kids" and not worry about their abuse or difficult lives at home for week or two each summer.

This is the dream we are going to make come true for her at Rachel's Ranch, a property we have purchased in Texas to build a camp where abused and disadvantaged kids can have a life experience they might not otherwise be privileged to enjoy.

Larry and I love Rachel – and all our 8 children – so very much. Rach is our baby, the one who was called by special nicknames by all the family, the one who lived at home the longest, the one with whom Larry and I got to spend the most time. There will forever be a hole in our hearts that can never be filled.

Rachel was, is, and always will be a great source of joy in my life. I look forward to the day when I can once again hold her in my arms. So one final quote comes to mind as I close this book. It provides some insight into how very much we miss our Rachel:

> *A wife who loses a husband is called a widow.*
>
> *A husband who loses a wife is called a widower.*
>
> *A child who loses his parents is called an orphan.*
>
> *But there is no word for a parent who loses a child. That's how awful it is.*
>
> *--Neugeboren (1976)*
> *Page 154*

Coming Soon!

Watch for the upcoming companion workbook
Life Lessons From Rachel's Little Quote Book
Anticipated Publish Date Fall 2011

This new book will be in workbook form and will provide exercises based on *Rachel's Little Quote Book* to help readers assess ways in which the application of some of Rachel's favorite quotes to their own lives will help them be more productive, have more fulfilling relationships, and find greater joy in living.

How You Can Help Build the Camp at Rachel's Ranch

Thank you so much for purchasing this book! Please tell your family and friends about the Camp at Rachel's Ranch and Rachel's desire to help abused and disadvantaged children. You can help by:

1. Booking your next family reunion, church youth group, quilting retreat, scrapping retreat, wedding or training session at Rachel's Ranch by going to **www.RetreatAtRachelsRanch.com**
2. Buy more copies of this book at Amazon.com or **www.RachelsLittleQuoteBook.org**
3. Download the book to your Kindle at Amazon.com or at Barnes and Noble.
4. Contribute to the development of the Camp at Rachel's Ranch with cash, your labor, or other donations at **www.CampAtRachelsRanch.org** . There's lots of work to be done.

If you'd like to come visit Rachel's Ranch, just give us a call at 903-729-2811 or find us on Facebook. We'd love to see you!

Jan and Larry Myers, Rachel's Mom and Dad

www.ingramcontent.com/pod-product-compliance
Lightning Source LLC
Chambersburg PA
CBHW071956070426
42453CB00008BA/806